POPULAR WILDFLOWERS

of Alberta

and the

Canadian

Rockies

NEIL L. JENNINGS

T0273491

RMB

This book, in great measure, is a distillation of a long string
of years and a whale of a lot of real estate over which
my wife Linda and I chased blooming wildflowers.
I am sure tickled she came along with me.
She found most of them anyway.
Thanks, darling.

Popular Wildflowers of Alberta and the Canadian Rockies
Copyright © 2020 by Neil L. Jennings
First Edition

For information on purchasing bulk quantities of this book, or to
obtain media excerpts or invite the author to speak at an event,
please visit rmbooks.com and select the "Contact" tab.

RMB | Rocky Mountain Books Ltd.
rmbooks.com
@rmbooks
facebook.com/rmbooks

Cataloguing data available from Library and Archives Canada
ISBN 9781771603492 (paperback)
ISBN 9781771603508 (electronic)

All photographs are by the author unless otherwise noted.

Printed and bound in Canada

We would like to also take this opportunity to acknowledge the traditional territories
upon which we live and work. In Calgary, Alberta, we acknowledge the Niitsitapi
(Blackfoot) and the people of the Treaty 7 region in Southern Alberta, which includes
the Siksika, the Piikuni, the Kainai, the Tsuut'ina and the Stoney Nakoda First Nations,
including Chiniki, Bearpaw, and Wesley First Nations. The City of Calgary is also home
to Métis Nation of Alberta, Region III. In Victoria, British Columbia, we acknowledge the
traditional territories of the Lkwungen (Esquimalt, and Songhees), Malahat, Pacheedaht,
Scia'new, T'Sou-ke and W̱SÁNEĆ (Pauquachin, Tsartlip, Tsawout, Tseycum) peoples.

We acknowledge the financial support of the Government of Canada through the Canada
Book Fund and the Canada Council for the Arts, and of the province of British Columbia
through the British Columbia Arts Council and the Book Publishing Tax Credit.

Disclaimer

It is up to the users of this guidebook to acquire the necessary skills for safe experiences
and to exercise caution. The author and publisher of this guide accept no responsibility for
your actions or the results that occur from another's actions, choices or judgments. If you
have any doubt as to the safety of any given plant, avoidance is the best course of action.

CONTENTS

ACKNOWLEDGEMENTS

I owe a debt of gratitude to a number of family members who contributed to this book by way of their continuous encouragement and support. Particular appreciation goes to my wife, Linda, who accompanied me on many flower outings and allowed me frequent absences from other duties in favour of chasing blooming flowers. My children, and, I am happy to say, their children, all deserve mention as well, given that they were often seconded to tramp around with me and bring me home alive. Thanks also go to many friends who encouraged me in my projects and often went into the field with me, according me a level of patience that was above and beyond the call of duty. I also wish to especially thank (or perhaps blame) the now departed S. Don Cahoon, who often shamed me with my ignorance and convinced me to educate myself about the beauty that resides in fields of wildflowers.

INTRODUCTION

This book is intended to be a field guide for the amateur naturalist to the identification of wild flowering plants commonly found in southern Alberta, southeastern British Columbia and several of the border states of the USA. This is not a book for scientists. It is for the curious traveller who wants to become acquainted with the flowers encountered during outings. The book differs from most other field guides in that it makes no assumption that the reader has any background in things botanical. It is also small enough to actually carry in the field and not be a burden. I believe most people want to be able to identify the flowers they encounter because this enriches their outdoor experience. Some might think it a difficult skill to perfect, but take heart and consider this: you can easily put names and faces together for several hundred family members, friends, acquaintances, movie stars, authors, business and world leaders, sports figures etc. Wildflower recognition is no different, and it need not be complicated.

For purposes of this book, the area of interest is loosely described as southern Alberta generally, from montane elevations upwards to the alpine community on the Rocky Mountains. Prairie species are addressed in a companion volume in this series, *Popular Wildflowers of the Canadian Prairies*.

The book does not cover all of the species of wildflowers and flowering shrubs that exist here, but it does include a large representation of the more common floral communities that might be encountered in a typical day during the blooming season. No book that I am acquainted with covers all species in any region, and indeed if such a source existed, it would be too large to be easily carried. Obviously, space will not permit a discussion of all such species, nor would it be pertinent for the amateur naturalist. The region harbours a vast diversity of habitat. In fact, for its relative size, the region is said to have some of the greatest diversity of plant species of any comparable area in North America.

"Do you know what this flower is called?" is one of the most often asked questions when I meet people in the field. Hopefully, this book will enable the user to answer this question. Identification of the unknown species is based on comparison of the unknown plant with the photographs contained in the book, augmented by the narrative descriptions associated with the species pictured. In many instances the exact species will be apparent, while in other cases the reader will be led to plants that are similar to the unknown plant, thus providing a starting point for further investigation. For the purposes of this book, scientific jargon has been kept to a minimum. I have set out to produce the best photographic representations I could obtain, together with some information about the plant that the reader might find interesting, and that might assist the reader in remembering the names of the plants. In my view, what most people really want to know about wildflowers is "what is this thing?" and "tell me something interesting about it." Botanical detail, while interesting and enlightening to some of us, will turn off many people.

The plants depicted in the book are arranged first by colour and then by family. This is a logical arrangement for the non-botanist because the first thing a person notes about a flower is its colour. All of the plants shown in the book are identified by their prevailing common names. Where I knew of other common names applied to any plant, I've noted them. I have also included the scientific names of the plants. This inclusion is made to promote specificity. Common names vary significantly from one geographic region to another, but scientific names do not. If you want to learn the scientific names of the plants to promote precision, that's fine. If not, no worries, but just be mindful that many plants have different common names applied to them depending on geography and local usage.

A few cautionary comments and suggestions

While you are outdoors, go carefully among the plants so as not to damage or disturb them. Stay on the established trails; those trails exist to allow us to view the natural environment without trampling it to death. Many environments are delicate and can be significantly damaged by indiscriminately tromping around in the flora.

Do not pick the flowers. Leave them for others to enjoy.

Do not attempt to transplant wild plants. Such attempts are most often doomed to failure.

Do not eat any plants or plant parts. Do not attempt to use any plants or plant parts for medicinal purposes. To do so presents a potentially significant health hazard. Many of the plants are poisonous – some violently so.

One final cautionary note: the pursuit of wildflowers can be addictive, though not hazardous to your health.

Neil L. Jennings
Calgary, Alberta

TERRITORIAL RANGE OF WILDFLOWERS

Blue *and* **Purple** Flowers

This section includes flowers that are predominantly blue or purple when encountered in the field, ranging from pale blue to deep purple and from light violet to lavender. Some of the lighter hues of blue and purple might shade into pinks, so if you do not find the flower you are looking for here, check the other parts of the book.

Common Butterwort

Pinguicula vulgaris

BLADDERWORT FAMILY

This small plant is one of only a few carnivorous ones in the region. It grows from fibrous roots in bogs, seeps and wetlands and along stream banks and lakeshores from valleys to the subalpine zone. The pale-green to yellowish leaves are basal, short-stalked, somewhat overlapping and curled in at the margins, forming a rosette on the ground. The leaves have glandular hairs on their upper surface that exude a sticky substance that attracts and then ensnares small insects. The flower is pale to dark purple and solitary atop a leafless stem.

Alpine Forget-Me-Not

Myosotis alpestris

BORAGE FAMILY

This beautiful, fragrant little flower is easily recognized by its wheel-shaped blue corolla and prominent yellow eye. It occurs, often in clumps, in moist subalpine and alpine meadows. The leaves are lance-shaped to linear. The lower leaves have short stems, but the upper ones are clasping. The stems are covered with long, soft hairs. The Alpine Forget-Me-Not is the state flower of Alaska.

Mertensia
(Low Lungwort)
Mertensia oblongifolia

BORAGE FAMILY

This plant of the sagebrush flats and open ponderosa pines blooms early in the spring, and the flower resembles oblong blue bells. The plants grow very near to the ground, with the flowers hanging down in clusters, first looking like oblong, blue capsules, then opening to be oblong, blue, bell-shaped flowers. The common name Lungwort is derived from Europe, this plant's flowers being similar to the European Lungwort, a plant thought to be good in the treatment of lung diseases.

Stickseed
(Western Stickseed)
Hackelia floribunda

BORAGE FAMILY

This hairy biennial or short-lived perennial has stiffly erect stems and grows to 1 m tall. The small, yellow-centred blue flowers occur in loose clusters on curving stalks near the top of the plant. The fruits are nutlets that are keeled in the middle and attached to a pyramid-shaped base. Each nutlet has rows of barbed prickles. While the flowers on this plant are lovely to look at, the prickles on the nutlets cling easily to fur, feathers and clothing, thus lending the plant its common name.

Blue Clematis
Clematis occidentalis

BUTTERCUP FAMILY

A plant of shaded riverine woods and thickets, the Clematis is a climbing, slightly hairy, reddish-stemmed vine that attaches itself to other plants by slender tendrils. The flowers have four to five sepals and are purplish to blue in colour, with dark veins. The flowers resemble crepe paper. The fruits are mop-like clusters of seeds, each of which has a long, feathery style. The Blackfoot called the plant "ghost's lariat," a reference to the fact that the vine would entangle their feet when they walked through it. Clematis often goes by the locally common name of Virgin's Bower.

Blue Columbine
Aquilegia brevistyla

BUTTERCUP FAMILY

This plant occurs in deciduous, coniferous and mixed woods, meadows and riverine environments, and grows to heights of 80 cm. The leaves are mostly basal and compound, with each having three sets of three leaflets. The flowers appear on tall stems that reach above the basal leaves. The flowering stems have a small number of smaller leaves, each with only three leaflets. The attractive flower can be nodding or ascending, with five yellowish or white sepals and five blue to purplish reflexed petals, each with a hooked, nectar-producing spur at its end. Columbines have a very distinctive floral structure and are usually unmistakable. Bumblebees and butterflies are drawn to Columbines to collect the nectar.

Jones's Columbine
Aquilegia jonesii

BUTTERCUP FAMILY

This small, rare and beautiful dwarf Columbine grows on rocky exposed slopes and limestone screes, and can only be found in Canada in Waterton Lakes National Park. Its hairy, bluish-green leaves are divided into small lobes, occurring in tufts near ground level. The flowers are solitary on the stem, and appear disproportionately large for the plant. Typical of Columbines, there are five blue, wing-like sepals and five blue, tube-shaped petals that flare at the open end and taper to a spur at the other end. Numerous stamens and five pistils extend from the centre of the flower.

Low Larkspur
Delphinium bicolor

BUTTERCUP FAMILY

This is a plant of open woods, grasslands and slopes that grows up to 40 cm tall from fleshy rootstock. It usually has a single flowering stem. Larkspurs are easily recognized for their showy, highly modified flowers. The irregular petals are whitish to bluish, with sepals that are blue to violet. The upper sepal forms a large, hollow, nectar-producing spur. The flowers bloom up the stem in a loose, elongated cluster. The common name is said to have originated because the spur on the flower resembles the spur on the foot of a lark. The plant is poisonous to cattle and humans.

Monkshood

Aconitum columbianum

BUTTERCUP FAMILY

A plant of moist mixed coniferous forests and meadows, Monkshood has a distinctive flower construction that is unmistakable. The dark-blue to purple flowers appear in terminal open clusters, and the sepals form a hood like those worn by monks. The long-stalked leaves are alternate and shaped like large maple leaves. The plant contains poisonous alkaloids that can cause death within a few hours.

Dwarf Sawwort (Purple Hawkweed)

Saussurea nuda subsp. *densa*

COMPOSITE FAMILY

This plant occurs on rocky slopes, ridges and screes from moderate to high elevations, and stands up to 20 cm tall. When first encountered, it appears to be some sort of thistle. The leaves are alternate, hairy, lance-shaped, sharp-pointed and crowded on the stem. The inflorescence is a dense, ball-like cluster on the end of the stem, from which protrude purple disc florets. The specific epithet, *nuda*, means "naked," which is puzzling given that the stem of the plant is not naked. The subspecies epithet makes more sense given the dense construction of the plant.

Prairie Crocus

Anemone patens
(also *Pulsatilla patens*)

BUTTERCUP FAMILY

This plant is widespread and common in grasslands, dry meadows and mountain slopes. It is usually one of the first wildflowers to bloom in the spring, and can occur in huge numbers. The flowers are usually solitary, various blues to purples in colour and cup-shaped. White varieties are sometimes seen. It is interesting to note that the flower blooms before the basal leaves appear. The plant has many basal leaves, palmately divided into three main leaflets and again divided into narrow linear segments. The leaves on the flower stem appear in a whorl of three.

Blue Sailors (Chicory)

Cichorium intybus

COMPOSITE FAMILY

This native of Eurasia grows up to 175 cm tall at low elevations on dry plateaus and in fields, grasslands and waste areas. The basal leaves are lance-shaped and strongly toothed to lobed. The flowers have sky-blue ray flowers and no disc flowers, and they occur singly or in small groups widely spaced on the long branches. The flowers open only in the daylight. The stems exude a bitter-tasting, milky juice when broken.

Parry's Townsendia

Townsendia parryi

COMPOSITE FAMILY

This tap-rooted, reddish-stemmed perennial blooms in the early spring, and appears on dry hills and gravelly slopes, along stream banks and in grassy areas from prairie to alpine elevations. Most of the leaves are basal and form a rosette at ground level. The stems, leaves and bracts are covered in white hairs. The relatively large flowers appear low to the ground on short stems, and they consist of broad ray flowers of violet to purple surrounding bright-yellow disc flowers. The Blackfoot boiled the roots of some *Townsendias* to make a concoction for treating ailments in horses.

Showy Aster

Aster conspicuus

COMPOSITE FAMILY

This plant is widespread and common at low to mid-elevations in moist to dry open forests, openings, clearings and meadows. The flowers are few to many composite heads on glandular stalks, with 15–35 violet ray flowers and yellow disc flowers. The stem leaves are egg-shaped to elliptical, with sharp-toothed edges and clasping bases. Some Indigenous peoples soaked the roots of the plant in water and used the decoction to treat boils. The leaves were also used as a poultice for that purpose.

Alpine Speedwell (Alpine Veronica)

Veronica wormskjoldii
(also *V. alpina*)

FIGWORT FAMILY

This erect perennial stands up to 30 cm tall, and occurs in moist meadows and along streams in the subalpine and alpine zones. The leaves are elliptical to egg-shaped, and occur in opposite pairs spaced along the stem. The stems, leaves and stalks of the flowers are covered with fine, sticky hairs. The flowers are numerous and occur at the top of the stem. The corolla has four united blue petals, which exhibit dark veins.

Blue-Eyed Mary

Collinsia parviflora

FIGWORT FAMILY

This small annual grows in moist to dry, shaded or open sites from the foothills to the montane zone. The branched stems are slender and weak, causing the plant to sprawl. The leaves are opposite, narrowly egg-shaped to linear, and tapered to the base and tip. The upper leaves often appear in whorls of three to five leaflets. The small flowers are pale blue to white and blue, and emerge from the axils of the upper leaves. The upper lip has two lobes, while the lower has three with the middle lobe being folded inwards.

Creeping Beardtongue

Penstemon ellipticus

FIGWORT FAMILY

One of the most handsome and conspicuous of the *Penstemons*, Creeping Beardtongue has large, lavender-coloured flowers which seem out of proportion to the low-growing plant. The plant grows in rocky crevices and on talus and cliffs in subalpine and alpine regions. When in bloom the flowers spill forth in amazing numbers, covering the leaves beneath in a blue-purple flood of colour.

In the spring the beautiful flowers festoon rocky outcrops along trails. The plant is also known by the very appropriate common name Rockvine Beardtongue.

Kittentails

Besseya wyomingensis

FIGWORT FAMILY

This small plant is an early bloomer, and is found from dry, open grasslands to subalpine rocky slopes. The leaves are mostly basal, oval to heart-shaped, toothed on the margins, and have long stalks. The stem has small, clasping leaves. The flowers are densely crowded in a spike atop the stem. The individual flowers consist of two or three green sepals, two purple stamens and a purple style with a button-shaped stigma. There are no petals. The whole plant is covered in fine white hairs.

Shrubby Penstemon (Shrubby Beardtongue)

Penstemon fruticosus

FIGWORT FAMILY

This plant grows in dry areas from the montane to the subalpine zones. It has woody stems and almost looks like a shrub, growing to 40 cm tall, hence the common name. The leaves are opposite, lance-shaped, shiny and evergreen, with the largest ones appearing at the base of the stem. The flowers are large and lavender to purplish-blue in colour. The flowers appear in a raceme in pairs on one side of the stem. The long, tubular flowers are often pollinated by bees and hummingbirds.

Small-Flowered Penstemon (Slender Beardtongue)

Penstemon procerus

FIGWORT FAMILY

This plant grows up to 40 cm tall at low to alpine elevations, usually in dry to moist open forests, grassy clearings, meadows and disturbed areas. Most of the blunt to lance-shaped leaves appear in opposite pairs up the stem. The small blue to purple flowers are funnel-shaped and appear in one to several tight clusters arranged in whorls around the stem and at its tip. The common name, Beardtongue, describes the hairy, tongue-like staminode (sterile stamen) in the throat of the flower.

Sticky Purple Geranium

Geranium viscosissimum

GERANIUM FAMILY

This is a plant of moist grasslands, open woods and thickets that can grow up to 60 cm tall. The flowers have large, showy, rose-purple to bluish petals that are strongly veined with purple. The long-stalked leaves are deeply lobed and split into five to seven sharp-toothed divisions, appearing in opposite pairs along the stem. There are sticky, glandular hairs covering the stems, leaves and some flower parts. The fruit is an elongated, glandular hairy capsule with a long beak shaped like a stork's or crane's bill.

Blue-Eyed Grass

Sisyrinchium angustifolium

IRIS FAMILY

These beautiful flowers can be found scattered among the grasses of moist meadows from low to sub-alpine elevations. The distinctively flattened stems grow to 30 cm tall, and are twice as tall as the grass-like basal leaves. The blue flower is star-shaped, with three virtually identical petals and sepals, each tipped with a minute point. There is a bright-yellow eye in the centre of the flower. The blossoms are very short-lived, wilting usually within one day, to be replaced by fresh ones on the succeeding day.

Wild Chives
Allium shoenoprasum

LILY FAMILY

Allium is the Latin name for garlic and designates all wild onions. Wild Chives grow in wet meadows, along stream banks and at lake edges. The small pink or purple flowers are upright on the top of a leafless stalk and are arranged in a densely packed ball. Wild Chives have round hollow leaves near the base and produce a very distinctive "oniony" odour when broken. Indigenous peoples harvested wild onion bulbs before the plants flowered, and used the bulbs as food, both raw and cooked.

Giant Hyssop
Agastache foeniculum

MINT FAMILY

A plant common in thickets and along streams, this mint is erect and grows to heights of up to 1 m. The stem is square in cross-section, typical of the mint family. The leaves are opposite, oval and coarse-toothed, with pointed tips. The blue to purple flowers are densely packed and appear in interrupted clusters along the top of the stem. Indigenous peoples used the leaves of the plant for making a tea and as a flavouring in foods. The flowers were often collected for medicine bundles.

Marsh Hedge Nettle

Stachys palustris

MINT FAMILY

A plant of wetland margins, stream banks, marshes and wet ditches, Marsh Hedge Nettle grows erect to heights of up to 40 cm. The stems are square, the leaves opposite and simple, lance-shaped and hairy. The flowers are pale purple and appear at the top of the spike, often in interrupted fashion.

The genus name, *Stachys*, is Greek for "spike," referring to the inflorescence type. The specific epithet, *palustris*, is Latin meaning "of wet places."

Wild Mint (Field Mint)

Mentha arvensis

MINT FAMILY

This plant inhabits wetland marshes, moist woods, stream banks and lake shores and sometimes lives in shallow water. The purplish to pinkish to bluish flowers are crowded in dense clusters in the upper leaf axils. The leaves are opposite, prominently veined and highly scented of mint if crushed. The stems are square in cross-section and hairy. The strong, distinctive taste of mint is from their volatile oils. The leaves have long been used fresh, dried or frozen as a flavouring and for teas.

Bladder Locoweed (Stalked Pod Crazyweed)

Oxytropis podocarpa

PEA FAMILY

This alpine plant grows high above timberline on gravelly slopes, from a stout taproot that produces a rosette of leaves that lies flat on the ground. The leaves are covered with silvery hairs, and consist of 11–23 short, linear leaflets. The flower stalks are leafless, and rise just above the leaves, terminating with two or three pale-purple, pea-like flowers about 2 cm long. Each flower has a dark-purple, hairy calyx, with a characteristic beaked keel formed from the two lower fused petals.

Showy Locoweed

Oxytropis splendens

PEA FAMILY

This attractive member of the pea family has silvery leaves growing from a branched, woody stock. The flower stalk is elongated and holds dense clusters of numerous flowers above the silvery leaves. The flowers are purple to bluish and shaped like other members of the pea family. Locoweeds are poisonous to cattle, horses and sheep because the plants contain an alkaloid that can cause the blind staggers, a condition that makes the animal behave in a crazy fashion, ergo *loco* in Spanish.

Silky Lupine

Lupinus sericeus

PEA FAMILY

A leafy, erect, tufted perennial with stout stems that appears in sandy to gravelly grasslands, open woods and roadsides, often growing in dense clumps or bunches. The plant grows up to 80 cm tall. The flowers are showy in long, dense terminal clusters, and display a variety of colours in blues and purples, occasionally white and yellow. The flowers have a typical pea shape, with a strongly truncated keel and a pointed tip. The leaves of *Lupines* are very distinctive, being palmately compound and alternate on the stem, with five to nine very narrow leaflets that have silky hairs on both sides.

Jacob's Ladder (Showy Jacob's Ladder)

Polemonium pulcherrimum

PHLOX FAMILY

This plant grows in dry, open, rocky environments in the montane to alpine zones. The leaves are distinctive, being pinnately compound, with 11–25 leaflets that are evenly spaced, resembling a tiny ladder. The leaf arrangement gives the plant its common name, a reference to the story in the Book of Genesis of how Jacob found a ladder to heaven. The pale- to dark-blue, cup-shaped flowers appear in an open cluster at the top of the stem and have a vivid orange ring at the base of the cup. The plant has a foul odour.

Sky Pilot (Skunkweed)

Polemonium viscosum

PHLOX FAMILY

This beautiful plant is closely related to Jacob's Ladder, and is found in the alpine zone, growing on exposed scree slopes. The leaves consist of numerous leaflets that are closely packed, short, whorled and fern-like. The leaves are covered with sticky hairs and have an odour of skunk, giving rise to one of the common names for the plant. The five-lobed blue flowers are funnel-shaped and appear in clusters. Inside the flower there is a circle of yellow stamens and a long, threadlike style. When you hike near these plants, the skunk smell is quite potent.

Shooting Star

Dodecatheon pulchellum

PRIMROSE FAMILY

This plant is scattered and locally common at low to alpine elevations in warm, dry climates, grasslands, mountain meadows and stream banks. The leaves are lance- to spatula-shaped and appear in a basal rosette. The singular to several purple to lavender flowers nod atop a leafless stalk, with corolla lobes turned backwards. The stamens are united into a yellow to orange tube from which the style and anthers protrude. A harbinger of spring, these lovely flowers often bloom in huge numbers, turning the grasslands to a purple hue.

Marsh Cinquefoil

Potentilla palustris

ROSE FAMILY

This plant inhabits bogs, marshes, streams and ponds from valleys to the subalpine zone. It grows from long, smooth rhizomes, creeping along the ground and rooting at the nodes. The leaves are usually smooth and pinnately compound, with five to seven obovate (teardrop-shaped) leaflets that are deeply toothed. While other members of the *Potentilla* family have yellow or white to cream-coloured flowers, Marsh Cinquefoil has purple to deep-red flowers. The flowers have an offensive, rotten odour that attracts insects as pollinators.

Bog Violet

Viola nephrophylla

VIOLET FAMILY

This beautiful small violet grows in moist meadows, on stream banks and in woods. The leaves and flower stalks arise from the base of the plant. The leaves are oval to kidney-shaped, smooth, and scalloped on the margins. The purple to blue flowers each have a spur 2–3 mm long. Violets are high in vitamins c and A and have been used as food since early Greek and Roman times. They are still cultivated for that purpose in some parts of Europe. The young leaves and flower buds may be used in salads or boiled.

Silky Phacelia (Silky Scorpionweed)

Phacelia sericea

WATERLEAF FAMILY

This spectacular plant grows on dry, rocky, open slopes at moderate to high elevations. The leaves are deeply divided into many segments and covered with silky hairs. The purple to blue flowers occur in clusters up a spike, resembling a bottle brush. The individual flowers are funnel-shaped, with long, purple, yellow-tipped stamens sticking out. The clusters of coiled branches resemble scorpion tails, thus the common name. The flowers of this plant are quite stunning, and having once seen them, one is unlikely to forget it.

Thread-Leaved Phacelia (Thread-Leaved Scorpionweed)

Phacelia linearis

WATERLEAF FAMILY

This annual species of *Phacelia* occurs in the southern part of the region, but is more common east of the coastal mountains. It grows to 50 cm tall and appears on dry plateaus and foothills. Its hairy, alternate leaves are thin and linear below, developing side lobes higher on the stem. The lavender to blue flowers are reasonably large and appear in open clusters from the leaf axils.

White, Green *and* Brown Flowers

This section includes flowers that are predominantly white or cream-coloured, green or brown when encountered in the field. Given that some flowers fade to other colours as they age, if you do not find the one you are looking for here, check the other parts of the book.

Alpine Bistort (Viviparous Knotweed)

Polygonum viviparum

BUCKWHEAT FAMILY

This plant grows up to 30 cm tall and is found in moist meadows and along stream banks in the subalpine and alpine zones. Its shiny, dark-green leaves are basal and lance-shaped. The flowers are small, white (sometimes pink) and occur in a cluster at the top of an upright spike. The lower flowers give way to small purplish bulblets, each of which is capable of producing a new plant. These bulblets actually germinate while still attached to the parent plant.

Cushion Buckwheat (Silver-Plant)

Eriogonum ovalifolium

BUCKWHEAT FAMILY

This mat-forming species can be found from prairie elevations to alpine ridges. Its sometimes large mats are distinctive and appealing to the eye on high, rocky ridges. The leaves are oval in shape and densely covered in silver woolly hairs, giving the plant an overall grey or silver appearance. The white to cream-coloured flowers occur in dense, rounded heads atop short, leafless stems that arise from the basal growth. The flower umbels in this species are simple, not compound as in most members of the genus.

Baneberry

Actaea rubra

BUTTERCUP FAMILY

This perennial grows up to 1 m tall in moist, shady woods and thickets, along streams and in clearings from low to subalpine elevations. The plant has one to several stout, upright, branching stems. Its coarse-toothed leaves are all on the stem and are divided two or three times into threes. The inflorescence is a dense, white, cone-shaped cluster of flowers that appears on top of a spike. The fruit is a large cluster of either shiny red or white berries. The leaves, roots and berries of this plant are extremely poisonous.

Globeflower

Trollius albiflorus

BUTTERCUP FAMILY

This plant grows from thick rootstock and fibrous roots, and is found in moist meadows, along stream banks and in open, damp areas in the subalpine and alpine zones. Its shiny, bright-green, mostly basal leaves are palmately divided into five to seven parts and deeply toothed. The few stem leaves are alternate and short-stalked. The flowers are made up of five to ten white sepals (which may have a pinkish tint on the outside) that surround a central core filled with numerous dark-yellow stamens. This plant contains a poisonous alkaloid.

Western Anemone (Chalice Flower)

Pulsatilla occidentalis (also *Anemone occidentalis*)

BUTTERCUP FAMILY

This plant is considered by many to be emblematic of wet alpine meadows and clearings. Its large, creamy-white flowers bloom early in the spring as the leaves are beginning to emerge. The entire plant is covered with hairs, which keep it protected in its cold habitat. Most of the leaves are basal, but there is a ring of feathery, grey-green stem leaves just below the flower. The flower is replaced by a clump of plumed seeds at the tip of the flowering stem. Some people refer to this stage as Hippies on a Stick.

Cow Parsnip

Heracleum lanatum

CARROT FAMILY

A denizen of shaded riverine habitat, stream banks, seeps and moist open woods, this plant grows to over 2 m tall. The flowers are distinctive in large, compound, umbrella-shaped clusters (umbels) composed of numerous white flowers, with petals in fives. The leaves, compound in threes, are usually very large, softly hairy, toothed and deeply lobed. This species is a favourite food of bears.

Large-Fruited Desert-Parsley

Lomatium macrocarpum

CARROT FAMILY

This stout, low-lying perennial grows from an elongated taproot and puts up a stem that branches near the base and grows up to 50 cm tall in dry or gravelly areas and on open slopes. Its hairy, clustered leaves are all basal, greyish in colour and finely dissected, resembling fern leaves. The white to purplish flowers occur in large umbrella-shaped clusters at the top of the multiple stems. The fruits are long and smooth, with narrow wings.

Water Hemlock

Cicuta maculata
(also *C. douglasii*)

CARROT FAMILY

This is a plant of marshes, river and stream banks and low, wet areas. It produces several large umbrella-like clusters (compound umbels) of white flowers appearing at the top of a sturdy stalk. The leaves are alternate and twice compound, with many lance-shaped leaflets. The primary lateral veins in the leaves end between the notched teeth on the leaflets rather than at their points. This is unique, and separates this species from parsley family members in the area.

While lovely to look at, the Water Hemlock is considered to be perhaps the most poisonous plant in North America. All parts of the plant are toxic, as testified to by several of its common names, including Children's Bane, Beaver Poison and Death of Man.

Ox-Eye Daisy

Leucanthemum vulgare

COMPOSITE FAMILY

An invasive Eurasian perennial from a well-developed rhizome, this plant frequents low to mid-elevations in moist to moderately dry sites such as roadsides, clearings, pastures and disturbed areas. The flowers are solitary composite heads at the end of branches, with white ray flowers and yellow disc flowers. The basal leaves are broadly lance-shaped or narrowly spoon-shaped. The stem leaves are oblong and smaller. This species is very prolific and will overgrow large areas if not kept in check. Many people consider it the most common and recognizable wildflower in North America.

Hooker's Thistle

Cirsium hookerianum

COMPOSITE FAMILY

This native thistle can grow up to 1 m tall, and is found in a variety of habitats from valleys up to alpine elevations. The flower heads are white, and the bracts surrounding the flowers point upward. The leaves, stems and bracts are all covered with silky hairs. The leaves display a prominent mid-vein. The species name celebrates Sir William Hooker, a prestigious English botanist. This plant was used as food by some Indigenous peoples, eaten either raw or cooked.

Yarrow

Achillea millefolium

COMPOSITE FAMILY

This is a plant of dry to moist grasslands, open riverine forests, aspen woods and disturbed areas. The individual white flower heads appear in a dense, flat-topped or rounded terminal cluster. The ray florets are white to cream-coloured (sometimes pink), and the central disc florets are straw-coloured. The leaves are woolly, greyish to blue-green and finely divided, almost resembling a fern. Yarrow can occur in large colonies. The genus name, *Achillea*, is in honour of Achilles, the Greek warrior.

Sticky Currant

Ribes viscosissimum

CURRANT FAMILY

This plant is a shrub that grows up to 2 m high in damp woods and clearings from valleys to subalpine elevations. It does not have prickles. The bell-shaped flowers are yellowish-white, often tinged with pink. The flowers and leaves are covered in glandular hairs that are sticky to the touch. The blue-black fruits also are sticky and not considered edible. The species name, *viscosissimum*, is derived from the Latin *viscosus*, meaning "sticky" or "viscid."

Bunchberry (Dwarf Dogwood)

Cornus canadensis

DOGWOOD FAMILY

This is a plant of moist coniferous woods, often found on rotting logs and stumps. The flowers are clusters of inconspicuous greenish-white flowers set among four white, petal-like showy bracts. The leaves are in a terminal whorl of four to seven, all prominently veined, and are dark green above, lighter underneath. The fruits are bright-red berries. The plant's common name, Bunchberry, is probably derived from the fact that the fruits are all bunched together in a terminal cluster when ripe.

Eyebright

Euphrasia nemorosa

FIGWORT FAMILY

These small, beautiful plants grow from a taproot that puts up slender, hairy, erect, sometimes branching stems that may reach 40 cm tall in moist woods at moderate to high elevations. The leaves are sessile (stalkless), egg-shaped to somewhat circular, sparsely hairy and glandular, and have decidedly toothed margins. The upper leaves are reduced in size, and the white flowers appear in the axils. The flowers are two-lipped, with the upper lip being bi-lobed and concave and the lower one having three spreading, notched lobes. There is purple pencilling on the lips and a yellow spot on the lower lip.

Sickletop Lousewort (Parrot's Beak)

Pedicularis racemosa

FIGWORT FAMILY

This lovely plant favours upper montane and subalpine environments. Its white flower has a very distinctive shape that deserves close examination to appreciate its intricacy. It is variously described as similar to a sickle, a tool with a short handle and a curved blade, or as resembling a parrot's beak, thus explaining the most often used common names. The flowers appear along a purplish stem that grows up to 35 cm tall. The leaves are simple, lance-shaped to linear and have distinctive fine, sharp teeth on the margins. Another locally common name for this plant is Leafy Lousewort.

White Geranium

Geranium richardsonii

GERANIUM FAMILY

This plant grows in moist grass-lands, open woods and thickets. It is very similar to Sticky Purple Geranium (*G. viscosissimum*) but has white to pinkish flowers with purple veins. The petals have long hairs at the base. The leaves are not sticky, and are hairy only along the veins on their lower sides. The fruits are capsules with long beaks shaped like a crane's or stork's bill. The fruit capsules are said to open explosively, with the beak splitting lengthwise from the bottom and catapulting the seeds away from the parent plant.

Fringed Grass of Parnassus

Parnassia fimbriata

GRASS OF PARNASSUS FAMILY

These plants abound in riverine habitat, pond edges and boggy places. The white flowers are very delicate looking. The flowers appear as singles on a slender stem, with five white petals and greenish or yellowish veins. The lower edges of the petals are fringed with hairs. Alternating fertile and sterile stamens are characteristic of this genus. The leaves are mostly basal and broadly kidney-shaped. A single leaf clasps the flowering stem about halfway up.

Labrador Tea

Ledum groenlandicum

HEATH FAMILY

This evergreen, much-branched shrub is widespread in low to subalpine elevations in peaty wetlands and moist coniferous forests. The flowers are white and numerous, with 5–10 protruding stamens in umbrella-like clusters at the ends of branches. The leaves are alternate and narrow, with edges rolled under. They are deep green and leathery on top, with dense rusty hairs underneath.

The fresh or dried leaves can be brewed into an aromatic tea, hence the common name. They were also used in barns to drive away mice and in houses to repel fleas.

One-Sided Wintergreen

Pyrola secunda
(also *Orthilia secunda*)

HEATH FAMILY

This small forest dweller grows to 15 cm tall at low to subalpine elevations in dry to moist coniferous or mixed woods and clearings. The white to yellowish-green flowers lie on one side of the arching stalk, arranged in a raceme of six to ten and sometimes more. The flowers resemble small street lights strung along a curving pole. The straight style sticks out beyond the petals, with a flat, five-lobed stigma. The egg-shaped, evergreen leaves are basal and fine-toothed at their margins. Once seen, this lovely little flower is unmistakable in the woods.

Single Delight (One-Flowered Wintergreen)

Moneses uniflora

HEATH FAMILY

This intriguing little forest dweller inhabits damp forests, usually on rotting wood. The plant is quite tiny, standing only 15 cm tall, and its single white flower, open and nodding at the top of the stem, is less than 5 cm in diameter. The flower looks like a small white umbrella offering shade. The leaves are basal, oval and evergreen, attached to the base of the stem. The style is prominent and tipped with a five-lobed stigma which almost looks like a mechanical part of some kind. The plant is also known locally as Wood Nymph and Shy Maiden.

White Mountain Heather

Cassiope mertensiana

HEATH FAMILY

This matting plant occurs in the subalpine and alpine zones. The flowers are white, bell-shaped and nodding at the end of the stems. The leaves are opposite, evergreen and pressed so close to the stems that the stems are all but hidden. The foliage forms low mats on the ground. The genus name originates in the Greek mythology surrounding Queen Cassiopeia and her daughter Andromeda.

While interesting, it is a complete mystery why Linnaeus chose the name. And by the way, all of the plants we North Americans call "heather" are not true heathers, but heaths.

White Rhododendron
Rhododendron albiflorum

HEATH FAMILY

This is an erect and spreading deciduous shrub that grows up to 2 m tall in cool, damp woods, often establishing dense communities under the conifer canopy. The leaves are oblong to lance-shaped and covered with fine rust-coloured hairs. The large, white, cup-shaped flowers are borne singly or in small clusters around the stem. They are also deciduous and fall from the plant intact, often littering the forest floor with what appear to be whole flowers. All parts of the plant contain poisonous alkaloids.

Red Twinberry (Utah Honeysuckle)
Lonicera utahensis

HONEYSUCKLE FAMILY

This erect deciduous shrub grows up to 2 m tall at low to subalpine elevations in moist to wet forest openings and clearings in the southern part of the region. The leaves are opposite and elliptical to oblong with smooth edges and blunt tips. The creamy-white flowers are trumpet-shaped and appear in pairs on a single stalk from the leaf axils. The fruits are red berries that are joined at the base. Some Indigenous peoples ate the berries, which were said to be a good emergency source of water because they are so juicy.

Beargrass
Xerophyllum tenax

LILY FAMILY

These impressive plants grow in peaty soil or clay in open woods and clearings from mid-elevations to the subalpine. The species has a basal clump of long, dense, sharp, evergreen leaves from which rises an impressive stem up to 150 cm tall. The inflorescence is a large torch-shaped cluster of hundreds of miniature white lilies which bloom from the bottom of the cluster first and then work their way upward. Individual plants may be sterile for several years, producing flowers only once to three times in a decade. Indigenous peoples used the leaves for weaving exquisite baskets, capes and hats.

Bronzebells
Stenanthium occidentale

LILY FAMILY

This lily of moist woods, stream banks, meadows and slopes has grass-like leaves that emerge from an onion-like bulb. The bell-shaped flowers are greenish-white flecked with purple, and have six sharp-pointed tips that twist backward, exposing the interior of the blossom. Ten or more graceful and fragrant flowers hang along the length of the stem, drooping down. Some authorities say this plant is poisonous; others say it is not.

Clasping-Leaved Twisted-Stalk

Streptopus amplexifolius

LILY FAMILY

This plant grows in moist, shaded forests, and has a widely branching zigzag stem with numerous sharp-pointed, parallel-veined leaves that encircle the stem at each bend. The glossy leaves often conceal the small, pale-white or greenish flowers that dangle on curving, threadlike stalks from the axil of each upper leaf. In fact, one could walk by the plant without even noticing its flowers, which appear to be hanging like small spiders dangling on fine webs. The fruits of this species are very handsome orangish-red, oval berries.

Death Camas (Meadow Death Camas)

Zigadenus venenosus (also *Toxicoscordion venenosum*)

LILY FAMILY

This plant of moist grasslands, grassy slopes and open woods grows from an onion-like bulb that has no oniony smell. The leaves are mainly basal and resemble grass, with prominent mid-veins. The greenish-white, foul-smelling flowers appear in tight clusters atop an erect stem, each flower having three virtually identical petals and sepals. There are yellowish-green, v-shaped glands (nectaries) near the base of the petals and sepals. The plant contains very poisonous alkaloids.

Fairybells
Prosartes hookeri
(form. *Disporum hookeri*)

LILY FAMILY

A plant of moist, shaded woods, stream banks and riverine environments, this delightful flower blooms in early summer. Its creamy-white, bell-shaped flowers have six tepals and occur in drooping pairs at the ends of branches. The leaves of the plant are generally lance-shaped, with parallel veins and pointed ends. The fruits are reddish-orange, egg-shaped berries occurring in pairs. The fruits are edible, but said to be bland. They are a favoured food of many rodents and birds.

Queen's Cup
Clintonia uniflora

LILY FAMILY

This beautiful perennial lily grows from slender rhizomes. The flowers are about 5 cm in diameter, and are usually solitary, white and cup-shaped, appearing at the top of an erect, hairy stem. The plant may display two or three shiny leaves at the base of its flowering stem, each of them oblong or elliptical with hairy edges. Its fruit is a single deep-blue berry, giving rise to two locally common names: Beadlily and Bluebead Lily.

Star-Flowered Solomon's Seal

Maianthemum stellatum

LILY FAMILY

This is a lily of moist woods, rivers and stream banks, thickets and meadows from montane to subalpine elevations. Its white, star-shaped flowers are arrayed in a loose, short-stalked cluster, often on a zigzag stem. The leaves are broadly lance-shaped, numerous and alternate, gradually tapering to a pointed tip, with prominent parallel veining, sometimes folded at the midline. The fruit is a cluster of green to cream-coloured berries with maroon to brown stripes.

Three Spot Mariposa Lily (Three Spot Tulip)

Calochortus apiculatus

LILY FAMILY

This is a plant of open coniferous woods; dry, sandy or gravelly slopes; and moist fescue grassland, from the montane to the subalpine zone. This perennial lily grows from a bulb to become a single-leafed plant that produces one to five flowers. The flowers are white to yellowish-white with three spreading petals fringed at the margins. Each petal is hairy on its inner surfaces and has a purplish gland at its base. These purple glands give the flower one of its common names, Three Spot Tulip. Three narrow white sepals appear between the petals.

Mariposa is Spanish for "butterfly."

White Camas

Zigadenus elegans (also *Toxicoscordion elegans*)

LILY FAMILY

This plant of moist grasslands, grassy slopes and open woods grows from an onion-like bulb that has no oniony smell. The greenish-white, foul-smelling flowers appear in open clusters along an erect stem. There are yellowish-green v-shaped glands (nectaries) near the base of the petals and sepals. The leaves are mainly basal and resemble grass, with prominent mid-veins. The species name, *elegans*, means "elegant." Though elegant indeed, these plants are extremely poisonous, containing very toxic alkaloids, particularly in the bulbs.

Other common names include Mountain Death Camas, Green Lily, Elegant Poison Camas, Elegant Death Camas and Showy Death Camas.

Heart-Leaved Twayblade

Listera cordata

ORCHID FAMILY

This small orchid, standing about 20 cm tall, prefers a cool, damp, mossy habitat. As a consequence of its size and preferred location, it is an easy flower to miss. Its white flowers are scattered up the stem in an open raceme. The lip of the flower is deeply split, almost in two. The stem leaf structure of the genus is distinctive, with two leaves appearing opposite each other partway up the stem. The specific epithet, *cordata*, means "heart-shaped," referring to the leaves.

Hooded Ladies' Tresses

Spiranthes romanzoffiana

ORCHID FAMILY

This orchid is reasonably common in swampy places, along lakeshores and in meadows and open, shady woods. It grows up to 60 cm tall. The characteristic feature of the plant is its crowded flower spike, which can contain up to 60 densely spaced white flowers that appear to coil around the end of the stem in three spiralling ranks. When newly bloomed, the flower has a wonderful aroma which most people say smells like vanilla. The common name is a reference to the braid-like appearance of the flowers, similar to a braid in a lady's hair.

Mountain Lady's Slipper

Cypripedium montanum

ORCHID FAMILY

This distinctive and relatively rare orchid grows up to 60 cm tall, occurring in dry to moist woods and open areas from mid- to subalpine elevations. Its lower petal forms a white, pouch-shaped lower lip that has purple markings. The brownish sepals and lateral petals have wavy margins and appear to spiral away from the stem. The attractive leaves are alternate, broadly elliptical and clasping on the stem, and have prominent veins. One to three flowers can appear on the stem, and they are wonderfully fragrant.

Round-Leaved Orchid
Amerorchis rotundifolia
ORCHID FAMILY

This tiny orchid, standing no more than 25 cm tall, occurs in well-drained parts of bogs and swamps and in cool, moist, mossy coniferous forests. The flowers are irregular, with three white to pink sepals. The upper sepal combines with the upper two, purple-veined petals to form a hood. The two lateral sepals are wing-like. The lowest petal forms an oblong lip that is white to pink and spotted with dark-red or purple markings. The leaf is basal, solitary and broadly elliptical. These small orchids are always a treat to discover, and in some places they appear in profusion.

Sparrow's-Egg Lady's Slipper (Franklin's Lady's Slipper)
Cypripedium passerinum
ORCHID FAMILY

This lovely orchid grows from a cord-like rhizome along streams and in boggy or mossy coniferous areas. It resembles other Lady's Slippers in shape, but this flower is decidedly smaller, with bright-purple dots on its interior, and has shorter, stubbier, greenish sepals. Both the stem and the leaves of the plant are covered in soft hairs. The species name, *passerinum*, means "sparrow-like," a reference to the spotting on the flower being like the markings on a sparrow egg.

Mealy Primrose

Primula incana

PRIMROSE FAMILY

This small plant inhabits moist meadows and slopes and the margins of sloughs and lakes, where it grows low to the ground with a basal rosette of leaves. The flowers are pale purple to white, with yellow centres. The petals are deeply notched and appear at the end of a tubular calyx. The common name refers to the mealy, cream-coloured scales on the undersides of the leaves. *Primula* is from the Latin *primus*, meaning "first," a reference to the early blooming time of many in the genus.

Sweet-Flowered Androsace (Rock Jasmine)

Androsace chamaejasme

PRIMROSE FAMILY

This striking, low-growing cushion plant is seldom more than 10 cm tall, but it can form mats of flowers on rocky ledges and in fields. The flowers are borne on a single white-hairy stem, and they occur in umbels of four to five flowers. The petals of the flowers are white, with a yellow or orange eye. Though small, these flowers have a wonderful aroma that is worth getting down on hands and knees to experience.

Small-Flowered Woodland Star (Woodland Star)

Lithophragma parviflorum

SAXIFRAGE FAMILY

This perennial grows up to 30 cm tall and occurs in low-elevation grasslands, open ponderosa pine stands and sagebrush areas. It blooms early in the spring. The leaves are mostly basal and kidney-shaped with deeply cleft and divided blades. The flowers are white to pinkish and occur in clusters at the tip of the stem. The flowers are broadly funnel-shaped, with five spreading, deeply lobed petals.

Western Canada Violet

Viola canadensis

VIOLET FAMILY

This plant favours moist to fairly dry deciduous forests, floodplains and clearings. The flowers are held on aerial stems and are white with yellow bases. The lower three petals have purple lines, while the upper two have a purplish tinge on the back. The leaves are heart-shaped, long-stalked and decidedly pointed at the tip, and have saw-toothed edges. This small, white flower splashes shady woods and marshes in midsummer. The plant grows from short, thick rhizomes with slender creeping runners. While easily propagated, they can become invasive in a garden setting.

Windflower

Anemone multifida

BUTTERCUP FAMILY

This plant favours south-facing slopes, grasslands and open woods. Like all anemones, Windflowers possess no petals, only sepals. The flowers are a variety of colours from white to yellowish to red, and appear atop a woolly stem. Beneath the flowers are bract-like leaves attached directly to the stem. The leaves are palmate, with deeply incised, silky-haired leaflets somewhat reminiscent of poppy leaves. The fruits are achenes in a rounded head, which later form a large, cottony mass. The common name, Windflower, comes from the method of distributing the long-plumed seeds of the plant.

Orange Agoseris (Orange-Flowered False Dandelion)

Agoseris aurantiaca

COMPOSITE FAMILY

This plant is relatively common in moist to dry openings, meadows and dry open forests in mid- to alpine elevations. Also known as False Dandelion, the plant occurs in yellow (*A. glauca*) as well as orange. Agoseris shares many characteristics with the Dandelion (*Taraxacum officinale*), but Agoseris is generally taller and its leaves are longer, with the leaf blades being smooth or faintly toothed rather than deeply incised the way the Dandelion's are. Some Indigenous peoples used the milky juice of the plant as a chewing gum. Infusions from it were also used for a variety of medicinal purposes.

Black Gooseberry (Swamp Currant)

Ribes lacustre

CURRANT FAMILY

This erect deciduous shrub grows to 150 cm tall in moist woods and open areas from foothills to the subalpine zone. The branches of the plant have small prickles and stout thorns at leaf and branch bases. The leaves are alternate and shaped like maple leaves, with three to five deeply cleft, palmate lobes. The reddish, saucer-shaped flowers hang in elongated clusters. The fruits are dark-purple to black berries that bristle with tiny hairs. The genus *Ribes* includes all Currants and Gooseberries. Gooseberries are bristly hairy, while Currants are not.

Spreading Dogbane

Apocynum androsaemifolium

DOGBANE FAMILY

This relatively common shrub occurs in thickets and wooded areas, and has freely branching, slender stems. The egg-shaped leaves are opposite and have sharp-pointed tips. The small, white to light-pinkish, bell-shaped flowers droop from the ends of the leafy stems, usually in clusters. The petal lobes are spreading and bent back, usually with dark-pink veins. Indigenous peoples used the tough fibres from these plants to fashion strong thread for making items like bowstrings and fishing nets. The pods of the plant are poisonous if eaten.

Fireweed (Great Willowherb)

Chamaenerion angustifolium (form. *Epilobium angustifolium*)

EVENING PRIMROSE FAMILY

This plant occurs in disturbed areas, roadsides, clearings and shaded woods from low elevations to the subalpine. It is often one of the first plants to appear after a fire. The pink, four-petalled flowers bloom in long terminal clusters. Bracts between the petals are narrow. The flowers bloom from the bottom of the cluster first, then upward on the stem. The leaves are alternate and appear whorled. Fireweed is the floral emblem of the Yukon.

River Beauty (Broad-Leaved Willowherb)

Chamaenerion latifolium (form. *Epilobium latifolium*)

EVENING PRIMROSE FAMILY

This plant grows as a pioneer, often in dense colonies, on gravelly floodplains and river bars, where the dense leaves and waving pink to purple flowers often obscure the stony ground underneath. River Beauty strongly resembles common Fireweed in appearance, but it has much shorter stems, broader leaves and larger, more brilliantly coloured flowers. The flowers bloom in a loose, short, leafy inflorescence. The leaves are bluish-green and waxy, with rounded tips. The plant is also known as Dwarf Fireweed.

Scarlet Butterflyweed

Gaura coccinea

EVENING PRIMROSE FAMILY

This is a plant of grasslands and dry, south-facing slopes. The flowers are whitish when they first bloom, becoming scarlet or pink as the flower ages. Usually only a few of the flowers on an individual plant bloom at once, and the flowers open fully only at night. The specific epithet, *coccinea*, means "scarlet," a reference to the colour of the flower. The common name arises most probably because the flowers are said to be shaped like butterflies.

Elephant's Head

Pedicularis groenlandica

FIGWORT FAMILY

This is a plant of wet meadows, stream banks and wetland margins. Its flowers appear in dense clusters atop a substantial stalk that can grow to 50 cm tall. Each of the flowers is reddish-purple to pinkish, and has an uncanny resemblance to an elephant's head, with a curved trunk and flared ears.

All members of this genus are somewhat parasitic on the roots of other plants, so transplantation is doomed to failure. When encountered, a close examination of this delightful flower is recommended, but be careful of the fragile habitat in which it lives.

Red Paintbrush

Castilleja miniata

FIGWORT FAMILY

A plant of alpine meadows, well-drained slopes, open subalpine forests, moist stream banks and open foothills woods, Paintbrush is widely distributed and extremely variable in colour. The leaves are narrow and sharp-pointed, linear to lance-shaped and usually without teeth or divisions, but sometimes the upper leaves have three shallow lobes. The showy red, leafy bracts, which are actually modified leaves, resemble a brush dipped in paint, hence the common name.

Red Monkeyflower (Lewis's Monkeyflower)

Mimulus lewisii

FIGWORT FAMILY

This plant occurs, often in large patches, along mountain streams and in other moist areas in the subalpine and alpine zones. The leaves are clasping, opposite and conspicuously veined, and have irregular teeth along their margins. The showy red flowers arise from the axils of the upper leaves. The flowers are funnel-shaped, with two lips which are hairy and have yellow markings.

Hummingbirds and bees are attracted to these flowers.

Thin-Leaved Owl's Clover

Orthocarpus tenuifolius

FIGWORT FAMILY

This plant grows up to 30 cm tall at low to subalpine elevations in dry grasslands and forests. The leaves are alternate, linear, unstalked and up to 5 cm long. The inflorescence is a dense, prominently bracted terminal spike. The petal-like bracts are broad, blunt-tipped and pinkish-purple in colour. Owl's Clovers are very similar to the Paintbrushes (*Castillejas*), but the latter are mostly perennial, while the Owl's Clovers are annuals.

False Azalea (Fool's Huckleberry)

Menziesia ferruginea (also *Rhododendron menziesii*)

HEATH FAMILY

This deciduous shrub is erect and spreading, and grows up to 2 m tall in moist, wooded sites from foothills to subalpine zones. The twigs of the shrub have fine, rust-coloured, sticky glandular hairs, and give off a skunky odour when crushed. The leaves are alternate, elliptical and glandular hairy, with a prominent mid-vein. The flowers are small, pinkish to greenish-orange and urn-shaped, nodding on long, slender stalks. The fruits are dark-purplish capsules which are inedible.

Kinnikinnick (Bearberry)

Arctostaphylos uva-ursi

HEATH FAMILY

This trailing or matted evergreen shrub grows low to the ground and has long branches with reddish, flaky bark and shiny-green, leathery leaves. The flowers are pale pink and urn-shaped, appearing in clumps at the ends of the stems. The fruits are dull-red berries. The berries are apparently relished by bears and birds, though they tend to be dry and mealy to humans. They are edible and have been used as food, prepared in a variety of ways. "Kinnikinnick" is believed to be of Algonquin origin and means "something to smoke," a reference to the use of the leaves of the plant as a tobacco.

Pink Wintergreen

Pyrola asarifolia

HEATH FAMILY

This plant is an erect perennial that inhabits moist to dry coniferous and mixed forests and riverine environments from the montane to the subalpine zone. Its waxy, pale-pink to purplish-red nodding flowers are shaped like an inverted cup or bell and have a long, curved, projecting style. The shiny, rounded, dark-green leaves are basal in a rosette and have a leathery appearance. The name "wintergreen" refers to evergreen leaves, not the flavour that has the same name.

Pipsissewa
(Prince's Pine)

Chimaphila umbellata

HEATH FAMILY

This small evergreen shrub grows to 30 cm tall in coniferous woods. Its glossy, dark-green leaves are narrowly spoon-shaped and saw-toothed and occur in whorls. The waxy pink flowers are saucer-shaped and nodding on an erect stem above the leaves. The fruits of the plant are dry, round, brown capsules that often overwinter on the stem. "Pipsissewa" is an adaptation of the Cree name for the plant.

Swamp Laurel
(Western Bog Laurel)

Kalmia microphylla

HEATH FAMILY

This low-growing evergreen shrub occurs in cool bogs and along stream banks and lakeshores in the subalpine and alpine zones. Its leathery leaves are dark-green above and greyish-white beneath, often with margins rolled under. The flowers are pink to rose-coloured, with the petals fused together to form a saucer or bowl on a reddish stalk. There are 10 purple-tipped stamens protruding from the petals. The leaves and flowers of this plant contain poisonous alkaloids that can be fatal to humans and livestock if ingested.

Twinflower

Linnaea borealis

HONEYSUCKLE FAMILY

This small trailing evergreen is common in coniferous forests, but is easily over-looked by the casual observer. The plant sends runners creeping along the forest floor, over mosses, stumps and fallen logs. At frequent intervals the runners give rise to distinctive Y-shaped stems 5–10 cm tall. Each fork of the stem supports at its end a pink to white, slightly flared, trumpet-like flower that hangs down like a small lantern on a tiny lamppost. The flowers have a sweet perfume that is most evident near evening.

Nodding Onion

Allium cernuum

LILY FAMILY

This plant is a common species in the region, and is easily identified by its smooth, leafless stem and drooping or nodding pink inflorescence. There are usually 8–12 flowers in the nodding cluster. The stem gives off a strong oniony odour when crushed. Indigenous peoples consumed the bulbs, both raw and cooked and as flavouring for other foods, and dried them for later use.

Sagebrush Mariposa Lily

Calochortus macrocarpus

LILY FAMILY

This is a large lily that occurs in the region in dry grasslands and open ponderosa forests. It has pinkish to purplish hues on the petals, which are decidedly pointed and display a crescent-shaped gland at the base of each one. This plant grows in more arid environments and blooms later than the Three Spot Mariposa Lily (*C. apiculatus*). The range of this plant has been severely restricted over the years by grazing cattle. The plant will not accept transplantation, so it is best to enjoy it in the wild where it grows.

Tiger Lily (Columbia Lily)

Lilium columbianum

LILY FAMILY

This showy lily can have up to 30 flowers per stem. The orange to orange-yellow blossoms hang downward, with reflexed petals, and have deep-red to purplish spots near the base. These spots are most probably the source of the common name Tiger Lily. The bulbs of the plants were used as food by some Indigenous peoples. They were said to have a peppery taste and would add that flavour to other foods. Overpicking has diminished the distribution of the plant.

Western Wood Lily

Lilium philadelphicum

LILY FAMILY

This lily grows in moist meadows and dense to open woods and at the edges of aspen groves from prairie elevations to the low subalpine zone. The leaves are numerous, lance-shaped, smooth and alternate on the stem, except for the upper leaves, which are in whorls. Each plant may produce from one to five bright-orange to orange-red flowers, each with three virtually identical sepals and petals. This plant is often confused with the Columbia Lily (*L. columbianum*) which is coloured similarly, but the tepals on the Columbia are reflexed, while the petals on the Wood Lily are held in a chalice shape.

Mountain Hollyhock

Iliamna rivularis

MALLOW FAMILY

This large plant can grow up to 2 m tall, and appears in montane to subalpine elevations on moist slopes and stream banks and in meadows. The leaves are fairly large, alternate and irregularly toothed, resembling maple leaves, with five to seven lobes each. The relatively large, pink to whitish, saucer-shaped flowers resemble garden Hollyhocks. They appear from the leaf axils along the stem and at the tips of the stems, in long, interrupted clusters. The flowers have many stamens, the filaments of which are united at the base to form a tube.

Spotted Coralroot (Summer Coralroot)

Corallorhiza maculata

ORCHID FAMILY

A plant of moist woods and bogs, this orchid grows from extensive coral-like rhizomes. There are no leaves, but the plant has several membranous bracts that sheath the purplish to brownish stem. A number of flowers appear on each stem, loosely arranged up the stem in a raceme. The three sepals and two upper petals are reddish purple. The lip petal is white with dark-red or purple spots and two lateral lobes. The plant lacks chlorophyll and does not produce food by photosynthesis, relying instead on parasitizing fungi in the soil.

Striped Coralroot

Corallorhiza striata

ORCHID FAMILY

This orchid grows from extensive coral-like rhizomes, and occurs in moist woods and bogs in the montane and subalpine zones. The pink to yellowish-pink flowers have purplish stripes on the sepals, and the lowest petal forms a tongue-shaped lip. A number of flowers appear on each stem, loosely arranged up the stem in an unbranched raceme. The leaves are tubular sheaths that surround, and somewhat conceal, the base of the purplish stem. The plant depends on a complex relationship with fungi in the soil for germination and survival.

Venus Slipper (Fairy Slipper)

Calypso bulbosa

ORCHID FAMILY

This orchid is found in moist, shaded coniferous forests. The flowers are solitary and nodding on leafless stems. The flower has pinkish to purplish sepals and mauve side petals. The lip is whitish or purplish with red to purple spots or stripes and is hairy yellow inside. The flower is on the top of a single stalk and has a deeply wrinkled appearance. This small but extraordinarily beautiful flower blooms in the early spring, often occurring in colonies.

Bitterroot

Lewisia rediviva

PURSLANE FAMILY

This is a plant of rocky slopes, dry grasslands and sagebrush slopes of the intermountain region. Its strikingly beautiful flowers are deep pink to sometimes white and have about 15 narrow petals. The flowers occur on such short stalks that they virtually appear to rest on the soil. The flowers only open in the sun. The leaves are all basal, appearing in the spring but withering and receding into the ground prior to the flower blooming. The Bitterroot was used as food and as a trading item by many Indigenous peoples.

Three-Flowered Avens (Old Man's Whiskers)

Geum triflorum

ROSE FAMILY

This plant is widespread in arid basins and on dry plateaus and open grasslands from prairies to subalpine elevations. The dull purplish to pinkish hairy flowers bloom in early spring, nodding at the top of the stem, usually in clusters of three though some plants can have as many as five on a single stem. The flowers remain semi-closed and do not open completely the way many common flowers do. The fruits are feathery clusters of brownish to purplish, plume-like achenes (small, dry, one-seeded fruits) that are sown by wind action. Indeed, when these seeds were being blown by the wind many early settlers referred to the phenomenon as "prairie smoke," accounting for another common name for the species.

Yellow Flowers

This section includes flowers that are predominantly yellow when encountered in the field. Their colours vary from bright yellow to pale cream. Some of the species included here have other colour variations, though, so you might have to check other parts of the book to find the one you're looking for. For example, the Paint-brushes (*Castilleja* sp) have a yellow variation but are most often encountered as red, so they are pictured in that section for purposes of sorting.

Oregon Grape

Mahonia nervosa

BARBERRY FAMILY

This evergreen shrub is widespread and common at low to mid-elevations on dry plateaus and in dry to moist forests and openings in the foothills. The plant very closely resembles holly, with shiny, sharp-pointed leaves that turn to lovely orange and rusty colours in the fall. The flowers are round and pale to bright yellow, and bloom in the early spring, giving way to a small purple berry that resembles a grape.

Puccoon (Lemonweed)

Lithospermum ruderale

BORAGE FAMILY

A coarse perennial up to 50 cm tall, this plant is firmly anchored to dry slopes and grasslands by a large, woody taproot. The numerous sharp-pointed leaves are lance-shaped and clasp the stem. The small yellow flowers are partly hidden in the axils of the leaves near the top of the plant, and have a strong, pleasant scent. The stems and leaves are covered in long white hairs. The fruit is an oval, cream-coloured nutlet that is somewhat pitted and resembles pointed teeth.

Yellow Buckwheat (Umbrella Plant)

Eriogonum flavum

BUCKWHEAT FAMILY

This fuzzy-haired, tufted perennial favours dry, often sandy or rocky outcrops, eroded slopes and badlands. The leaves are dark green on top, but appear white and felt-like on the underside due to the dense hairs. The yellow flowers occur in umbrella-shaped clusters – compound umbels – atop the stem. The common name, Umbrella Plant, is testimony to the shape of the inflorescence.

Alpine Buttercup

Ranunculus eschscholtzii

BUTTERCUP FAMILY

This plant can grow to heights of 30 cm near or above timberline, appearing beside streams or ponds, near snowdrifts and around late snowmelt. The leaves are mainly basal, sometimes deeply lobed, and round to kidney-shaped. The flowering stems are hairless, and may accommodate up to three flowers. The flowers are bright yellow, with five petals and five purple-tinged sepals. Stamens and pistils are numerous. The genus name, *Ranunculus*, is derived from the Latin *rana*, which means "frog," a reference to the wet habitat preferred by many members of the genus.

Marsh Marigold
Caltha palustris

BUTTERCUP FAMILY

Favouring wet meadows, woods and bogs, this plant is often found in shallow water of slow-moving streams and ditches. The flower has five to nine bright-yellow showy sepals, but no petals. Its large leaves are mostly basal and quite distinctive, being dark green and round to kidney- or heart-shaped. The common name is said to have come from "Mary's Gold," a reference to a yellow flower esteemed by the Virgin Mary. All parts of the mature plant are poisonous, but they are said to be distasteful to livestock because of the acrid juice.

Sagebrush Buttercup
Ranunculus glaberrimus

BUTTERCUP FAMILY

This beautiful little buttercup is one of the earliest-blooming wildflowers in the region, with its bright-yellow, shiny petals peeping out from the dead winter grasses of early spring on arid hillsides. The leaves are mainly basal and elliptical to lance-shaped. The flowers appear in patches or as single blooms. Sagebrush Buttercups are poisonous, containing an acrid alkaloid, and some Indigenous peoples warned their children not to touch or pick them.

Meadow Buttercup

Ranunculus acris

BUTTERCUP FAMILY

Among the tallest of the Butter-cups, this plant may reach almost 1 m in height. It is a hairy peren-nial, with broad leaves that are deeply lobed and divided nearly to the base. The flowers are glossy yellow, with greenish, hairy sepals that fall off soon after the flower blooms. The species name, *acris*, means "acrid," referring to the juice of this plant. All of the Buttercups contain poisonous compounds.

Yellow Columbine

Aquilegia flavescens

BUTTERCUP FAMILY

Lemon-yellow in colour, these beautiful flowers nod at the ends of slender stems that lift the flowers above the leaves. Each flower is composed of five wing-shaped sepals, and five tube-shaped petals that are flaring at the open end and tapering to a distinctive spur at the opposite end. The leaves are mainly basal, with long stems, and are deeply lobed. The plant occurs on rockslides and talus slopes and in meadows in the alpine and subalpine zones.

Heart-Leaved Alexanders (Meadow Parsnip)

Zizia aptera

CARROT FAMILY

This is a plant of prairies, moist meadows, open woods, stream banks and wetland margins. The small, bright-yellow flowers are numerous, and occur in compound, flat-topped clusters at the top of the stems. The lower leaves are leathery, dark green and heart-shaped. The stem leaves are smaller and divided into three leaflets. The stem leaves become progressively smaller along the stem until they become cleft leaflets. The flowers appear on top of hollow stems that are erect and reach heights of up to 60 cm.

Alpine Goldenrod

Solidago multiradiata

COMPOSITE FAMILY

This erect plant grows from a woody rootstock on dry, open slopes in the subalpine and alpine zones. The leaves are alternate, and often have a reddish appearance. The basal leaves and lower stem leaves are broadly lance- or spoon-shaped and slightly toothed, with hairy margins. The flowers are yellow and occur in loose or dense, narrow, long clusters atop the stem. Each flower is composed of 8 ray florets, surrounding 13 or more disc florets.

Annual Hawk's Beard

Crepis tectorum

COMPOSITE FAMILY

A plant of moist open areas and saline meadows, this annual will grow up to 1 m tall. The basal leaves usually wither before flowering occurs. The stems have a few thin, alternate leaves. Each plant will produce a few to 15 yellow flowers composed of yellow ray flowers, but no disc flowers. The fruits of the plant are dark-purplish-brown achenes with a pappus of fine, white, hair-like bristles at the top.

Arrow-Leaved Balsamroot

Balsomorhiza sagittata

COMPOSITE FAMILY

This is a widespread and frequently abundant plant of hot, arid climates, often found on rocky, south-facing slopes. Its flowers are solitary composite heads with bright-yellow ray flowers and yellow disc flowers, and are densely hairy, especially at the base. The large, silvery leaves are arrowhead-shaped and covered with dense, felt-like hairs. Balsamroot often provides a showy early-spring splash of colour on warm, dry hillsides. All parts of the plant are edible, and the species was an important food for Indigenous peoples.

Arrow-Leaved Groundsel (Giant Ragwort)

Senecio triangularis

COMPOSITE FAMILY

This perennial will grow to 150 cm tall, often in large clumps in moist to wet open or partly shaded sites from foothills to alpine elevations. The leaves are alternate, spearhead or arrowhead in shape, squared off at the base and tapered to the point. The leaves are numerous, coarse-toothed and well developed along the whole stem of the plant. The flowers occur in flat-topped clusters at the top of the stem and have five to eight bright-yellow ray florets surrounding a disc of bright-yellow to orange florets.

Black-Tipped Groundsel

Senecio lugens

COMPOSITE FAMILY

This is a perennial that occurs on moist subalpine slopes and in alpine meadows. The leaves are mostly clustered at the base, surrounding the stem. The flowers are typical of the Groundsels – bright-yellow, lance-shaped ray florets surrounding yellow to orange disc florets. The bracts below the flowers have conspicuous black tips, a useful feature in the identification of the species. The bracts on other Groundsels are green.

Brown-Eyed Susan (Gaillardia)

Gaillardia aristata

COMPOSITE FAMILY

This is a plant of open grasslands, dry hillsides, roadsides and open woods. The flowers are large and showy, with yellow ray florets that are purplish to reddish at the base. The central disc is purplish and woolly hairy. The leaves are numerous, alternate and lance-shaped, usually looking greyish and rough owing to the many short hairs. A number of Indigenous peoples used the plant to relieve a variety of ailments.

Golden Fleabane

Erigeron aureus

COMPOSITE FAMILY

This plant is a dwarf perennial that occurs in the alpine zone, growing on turf slopes. The deep-green, oval leaves are on short stalks, and form a rosette on the ground. The yellow flowers have 25–70 ray florets surrounding yellow disc florets, and appear singly on mostly leafless stems that grow up to 15 cm high. The bracts on the flower heads are covered with woolly hairs and have a purplish tip.

Heart-Leaved Arnica

Arnica cordifolia

COMPOSITE FAMILY

Arnica is a common plant of wooded areas in the mountains, foothills and boreal forest. The leaves occur in two to four opposite pairs along the stem, each with long stalks and heart-shaped, serrated blades. The uppermost pair is stalkless and more lance-shaped than the lower leaves. The flowers have 10–15 bright-yellow ray florets and bright-yellow central disc florets.

Late Goldenrod

Solidago gigantea

COMPOSITE FAMILY

This plant appears in moist woods and meadows and on floodplains and lakeshores. The flowers are bright yellow, terminal, broadly pyramidal clusters of flower heads. The leaves are numerous, alternate, thin and lance-shaped, tapering to the base. The genus name, *Solidago*, is probably from the Latin *solidus*, meaning "whole" and *ago*, meaning "to put in motion" or "to conduct," because of the plant's healing properties. Some Indigenous peoples ground the flowers into a lotion and applied it to bee stings.

Lyall's Iron Goldenweed (Lyall's Iron Plant)

Haplopappus lyallii

COMPOSITE FAMILY

This small perennial grows to heights of 15 cm from a taproot secured in meadows and on scree slopes and gravelly ridges in the alpine zone. The leaves are stemless, lance-shaped and hairy, glandular, and covered in a sticky coating. In addition, the leaves are clumped at the base of the flower stem and extend up the stem. The yellow flower is a solitary composite head with up to 35 ray flowers and yellow disc flowers.

Pineapple Weed (Disc Mayweed)

Matricaria discoidea

COMPOSITE FAMILY

This branching annual grows up to 40 cm tall along roadsides, in ditches and on disturbed ground. The stem leaves are alternate and fern-like, with finely dissected, narrow segments. Basal leaves have usually fallen off by the time flowering occurs. The flowers are several to many composite heads, with greenish to yellow disc florets on a cone- or dome-shaped base. There are no ray florets. When crushed, the leaves and flowers of the plant produce a distinctive pineapple aroma, hence the common name.

Prairie Coneflower

Ratibida columnifera

COMPOSITE FAMILY

This is a plant of dry grasslands, coulees and disturbed areas that can reach heights of up to 60 cm. Its greyish-green leaves are alternate and deeply divided into oblong lobes. The distinctive flower appears atop a tall, slender stem, and consists of dark-purple disc florets formed into a cylinder up to 4 cm long, the base of which is surrounded by bright-yellow ray florets. The origin of the genus name, *Ratibida*, is unknown. The species name, *columnifera*, is a reference to the column or cone-shaped inflorescence.

Prairie Groundsel
Senecio canus

COMPOSITE FAMILY

This is a white, woolly perennial that can stand up to 40 cm in height. It occurs at a variety of elevations from prairie to almost timberline. The leaves are clustered at the base, with taller stems supporting the flowers. Stem leaves are alternate and diminishing in size as the stem rises. All leaves are greyish green and covered with fuzzy white hairs. The yellow flower heads are solitary to several on a stem, with notched ray florets surrounding a cluster of disc florets.

Prickly Lettuce
Lactuca serriola

COMPOSITE FAMILY

This plant grows in fields and disturbed areas at low to mid-elevations. The leaves are once or twice lobed, and prickly on the sides. The flowers have composite heads, with yellow ray flowers and no disc flowers. Prickly Lettuce is an introduced species, having come from Europe. It has become an invasive weed in many areas of North America. The plant will exude a milky sap when the stem is broken.

Slender Hawkweed

Hieracium gracile

COMPOSITE FAMILY

This plant is common to open woods, meadows, roadsides, ditches and disturbed areas. The yellow flower heads appear in a cluster on ascending stalks. The flowers are composed entirely of ray florets; there are no disc florets. The leaves are in a basal rosette, broadly lance-shaped to spoon-shaped. The genus name, *Hieracium*, is from the Greek *hierax*, meaning "hawk," as it was once believed that eating these plants improved a hawk's vision. The leaves, stems and roots produce a milky latex that was used as a chewing gum by some Indigenous peoples.

Sow Thistle (Perennial Sow Thistle)

Sonchus arvensis

COMPOSITE FAMILY

This is a plant of cultivated fields, roadsides, ditches and pastures. The flowers have large yellow ray florets similar to dandelion flowers. Sow Thistle is an imported species from Europe and is not a true thistle. Sow Thistles will exude a milky latex when the stem is crushed, while true thistles do not. The common name is derived from the fact that pigs like to eat this plant.

Bracted Lousewort (Wood Betony)

Pedicularis bracteosa

FIGWORT FAMILY

This plant can attain heights of up to 1 m, and is found at subalpine and alpine elevations in moist forests, meadows and clearings. Its fern-like leaves are divided into long, narrow, toothed segments and are attached to the upper portions of the stem of the plant. The flowers, varying from yellow to red to purple, arise from the axils of leafy bracts and occur in an elongated cluster at the top of the stem. They have a two-lipped corolla, giving the impression of a bird's beak.

Yellow Beardtongue (Yellow Penstemon)

Penstemon confertus

FIGWORT FAMILY

This is a plant of moist to dry meadows, woodlands, stream banks, hillsides and mountains. The small, pale-yellow flowers are numerous and appear in whorled, interrupted clusters along the upper part of the stem. Each flower is tube-shaped and has two lips. The lower lip is three-lobed and bearded at the throat, while the upper one is two-lobed. The common name, Beardtongue, describes the hairy, tongue-like staminode (sterile stamen) in the throat of the flower. The genus name, *Penstemon*, is a reference to the five stamens in the flower.

Yellow Monkeyflower

Mimulus guttatus

FIGWORT FAMILY

This plant occurs, often in large patches, along streams, at seeps and in moist meadows. The species is quite variable, but is always spectacular when found. The bright-yellow flowers resemble Snapdragons and occur in clusters. They usually have red or purple dots on the lip, giving the appearance of a grinning face. The genus name, *Mimulus*, is derived from the Latin *mimus*, meaning "mimic" or "actor."

Golden Corydalis

Corydalis aurea

FUMITORY FAMILY

This plant of open woods, roadsides, disturbed places and stream banks is an erect or spreading, branched, leafy biennial or annual. It germinates in the fall and overwinters as a seedling. In the spring, it grows rapidly, flowers and then dies. The yellow flowers are irregularly shaped, rather like the flowers of the pea family, with keels at the tips. A long, nectar-producing spur extends backward from the upper petal.

Yellow Heather (Yellow Mountain Heather)

Phyllodoce glanduliflora

HEATH FAMILY

This dwarf evergreen shrub grows up to 30 cm high, and thrives in subalpine and alpine meadows and slopes near timberline. The flowers, stems and new growth are covered with small sticky hairs. The blunt, needle-like leaves are grooved on their undersides. The yellowish-green, vase- or urn-shaped flowers are nodding in clusters at the top of the stems.

Black Twinberry (Bracted Honeysuckle)

Lonicera involucrata

HONEYSUCKLE FAMILY

This plant is a shrub that grows up to 2 m tall in moist woods and along stream banks. Its yellow flowers occur in pairs arising from the axils of the leaves, and are over-lain by a purple to reddish leafy bract. As the fruit ripens the bract remains, enlarges and darkens in colour. The ripe fruits occur in pairs and are black. They are bitter to the taste, but serve as food for a variety of birds and small mammals.

Twining Honeysuckle
Lonicera dioica

HONEYSUCKLE FAMILY

This plant is a flowering vine of the Rocky Mountains that clambers over low bushes and shrubs and around tree trunks at low elevations. The trumpet-shaped flowers cluster inside a shallow cup formed by two leaves that are joined at their bases. The cupped leaves are very distinctive and are referred to as "connate" leaves. When the flowers first appear they are yellow, turning orange to brick colour with age. The five petals are united into a funnel-shaped tube which has a swollen knob near the base where nectar is accumulated.

Glacier Lily (Yellow Avalanche Lily)
Erythronium grandiflorum

LILY FAMILY

This gorgeous lily is one of the first blooms in the spring, often appearing at the edges of receding snowbanks on mountain slopes, thus the common names. The bright-yellow flowers that appear at the top of the leafless stem are usually solitary, though a plant might have up to three flowers. The flowers are nodding, with six tepals that are tapered to the tip and reflexed, with white, yellow or brown anthers. The broadly oblong, glossy leaves, usually two, are attached near the base of the stem and are unmarked.

Yellowbell

Fritillaria pudica

LILY FAMILY

This diminutive flower is a harbinger of spring, often blooming just after snowmelt in dry grasslands and dry, open ponderosa pine forests. It can easily be overlooked because of its small size, usually standing only about 15 cm tall. The yellow, drooping, bell-shaped flowers are very distinctive. The flowers turn orange to brick-red as they age. The leaves, usually two or three, are linear to lance-shaped, and appear more or less opposite about halfway up the stem. The Yellowbell sometimes appears with two flowers on a stem, but single blooms are more common.

Douglas Maple (Rocky Mountain Maple)

Acer glabrum

MAPLE FAMILY

This deciduous shrub or small tree is found in moist, sheltered sites from foothills to subalpine zones. The plant has graceful, wide-spreading branches. The young twigs are smooth and cherry-red, turning grey with age. The leaves are opposite and typical of maples: three-lobed, with an unequal and sharp-toothed margin. The yellowish-green flowers are short-lived and fragrant, with five petals and five sepals, hanging in loose clusters. The fruits are v-shaped pairs of winged seeds joined at the point of attachment to the shrub. The fruit is known as a "samara."

Golden Draba (Yellow Draba, Golden Whitlow Grass)

Draba aurea

MUSTARD FAMILY

This mustard grows up to 50 cm tall, and occurs on rocky slopes and in open woods and meadows from the montane to the alpine zones. Its hairy basal leaves are lance-shaped and appear in a rosette. The stalkless, hairy, lance-shaped stem leaves are alternate, somewhat clasping, and distributed up the stem. The bright-yellow flowers are four-petalled and appear in a cluster at the top of the stem. Mustards typically have four petals in a cruciform shape.

Soopolallie (Canadian Buffaloberry)

Shepherdia canadensis

OLEASTER FAMILY

This deciduous shrub grows up to 3 m tall, and is often the dominant understorey cover in lodgepole pine forests. All parts of the plant are covered with rust-coloured, shiny scales, giving the whole plant an orange, rusty appearance. The leaves are leathery and thick, green and glossy on the upper surface, while the lower surface is covered with white hairs and sprinkled with rusty-coloured dots. The male and female flowers appear on separate plants. The small, inconspicuous yellow flowers often appear on the branches of the plant prior to the arrival of the leaves.

Wolf Willow (Silverberry)

Elaeagnus commutata

OLEASTER FAMILY

This deciduous shrub grows up to 4 m tall, often in dense stands. Its twigs are thickly covered with rusty-brown scales, while its oval, silvery leaves are alternate and similarly covered with small scales. The flowers are funnel-shaped and have four yellow lobes, occurring at the leaf axils. The flowers are very fragrant with a distinctive aroma. The fruits are silvery, round to egg-shaped berries and usually persist throughout the winter.

Pale Coralroot

Corallorhiza trifida

ORCHID FAMILY

This orchid is found in moist woods and bogs, growing to heights of about 15 cm from extensive coral-like rhizomes. The cream to greenish-yellow flowers are spread out along the thick stalk, in a cluster at the top of the stem. The flowers often have pale red dots on the lip. All Coralroots are saprophytes, i.e., plants that lack any of the green pigment (chlorophyll) used by most plants for food production. Instead, it absorbs its nutrition from decaying organic matter in the soil.

Yellow Lady's Slipper

Cypripedium parviflorum

ORCHID FAMILY

This is an orchid of bogs, damp woods and stream banks. The leaves are alternate, with two to four per stem, broadly elliptical, and clasping. The yellow flowers usually occur as a single on a stem, and resemble a small shoe. The sepals and lateral petals are similar, greenish-yellow to brownish, with twisted, wavy margins. The lower petal forms a prominent pouch-shaped yellow lip with purple dotting around the puckered opening. This flower has suffered large range reductions as a result of picking and attempted transplantation, which almost always fails.

Buffalo Bean (Golden Bean)

Thermopsis rhombifolia

PEA FAMILY

This plant occurs on grassy hillsides, roadsides, ditches and prairies, often forming large clumps. Its bright-yellow flowers bloom in crowded clusters atop the stem, which grows to 35 cm tall. The flower has the typical pea shape, with the keel enclosing the stamens. The leaves are opposite, alternate, compound and clasping leaflets. The plant takes its common name from Blackfoot parlance. The Blackfoot took the flower's blooming as a sign to go hunting buffalo, the buffalo having fattened on spring grasses. Buffalo did not eat these flowers, though, because the plant contains poisonous alkaloids.

Field Locoweed

Oxytropis campestris

PEA FAMILY

This early-blooming plant is widespread and common in rocky outcrops, roadsides and dry open woods in the region. The leaves are mainly basal, with elliptical leaflets and dense hairs. The pale-yellow, pea-like flowers bloom in clusters at the top of a leafless, hairy stem. The plant is poisonous to cattle, sheep and horses, owing to its high content of alkaloids that cause blind staggers. This loss of muscle control in animals that have ingested this plant is the origin of the common name for the flower, *loco* being Spanish for "crazy" or "foolish."

Yellow Hedysarum

Hedysarum sulphurescens

PEA FAMILY

This is a plant of stream banks, grasslands, open forests and clearings. Its yellowish to nearly white flowers are pea-like and drooping, usually appearing along one side of the stem in elongated clusters (racemes). The fruits of the plant are long, flat, pendulous pods with conspicuous winged edges and constrictions between each of the seeds. This plant is also called Yellow Sweet Vetch. It is an extremely important food for grizzly bears, which eat the roots in the spring and fall.

Antelope Brush (Pursh's Bitterbrush)

Purshia tridentata

ROSE FAMILY

This deciduous shrub grows on dry sites in plains and foothills and reaches heights of up to 2 m. The plant is rigidly branched and the branches are covered with dense, woolly hairs. The flowers are numerous, funnel-shaped and bright yellow, appearing from the branches of the shrub, usually in the spring. Antelope Brush is important browse for deer and elk, and the seeds from the plant are favourites of small burrowing mammals like chipmunks, ground squirrels and mice.

Early Cinquefoil

Potentilla concinna

ROSE FAMILY

This plant is a very short, spreading perennial that supports two to five flowers per plant. The flowers are bright yellow, with five rounded petals, appearing as solitary flowers atop a leafless stem. The plant is usually less than 10 cm tall and blooms early in the spring, usually in dry, sandy soil. Indeed, it is often one of the first flowers seen in the spring.

Shrubby Cinquefoil

Potentilla fruticosa

ROSE FAMILY

This low deciduous shrub is found on rocky slopes and in dry meadows and gravelly river courses at low to subalpine elevations. Its leaves are alternate, divided into three to seven (usually five) greyish-green leaflets that are lightly hairy and often have curled edges. The flowers are golden yellow and saucer-shaped, with five rounded petals, usually blooming as a solitary at the end of branches. The flowers are often smaller and paler at lower elevations, larger and brighter in higher terrain. Many *Potentilla* species have five leaflets and the flower parts are in fives.

Sibbaldia

Sibbaldia procumbens

ROSE FAMILY

This is a ground-hugging alpine-zone perennial that forms cushions. Its prostrate stems branch from the base and terminate in clusters of three leaflets, similar to clover. White hairs cover both surfaces of the leaflets. The pale-yellow flowers are generally saucer-shaped and appear in clusters at the tops of the flowering stems. Each flower is made up of five yellow petals that alternate with five hairy green sepals. The petals are about half as long as the sepals.

Sticky Cinquefoil
Potentilla glandulosa

ROSE FAMILY

This plant inhabits open forests and meadows at low to mid-elevations. It grows to about 40 cm tall from a branched rootstock, and the leaves and stems are covered with glandular hairs that exude a sticky, aromatic fluid. The leaves are mainly basal and pinnately divided into five to nine sharp-toothed oval leaflets. The flowers are typical of the *Potentillas* and are pale yellow to creamy white, occurring in small, open clusters at the top of the stems.

Yellow Avens
Geum aleppicum

ROSE FAMILY

This plant is an erect, hairy, tall perennial that grows in moist woods and thickets and along rivers and streams. The flowers are bright yellow and saucer-shaped, with five petals. The flowers usually appear at the tip of a tall, slender stem. The basal leaves of the plant occur in a cluster and are compound and toothed. The top leaflet is heart- to kidney-shaped and deeply lobed.

Yellow Mountain Avens (Drummond's Mountain Avens)

Dryas drummondii

ROSE FAMILY

This is a plant of gravelly streams and riverbanks, slopes and road-sides in foothills and mountains. The yellow flower is solitary and nodding, with black, glandular hairs, blooming on the top of a hairy, leafless stalk. Leaves are alternate, leathery and wrinkly, dark green above and whitish-hairy beneath. The fruit consists of many achenes, each with a silky, feathery, golden-yellow plume that becomes twisted around the others into a tight spiral that later opens into a fluffy mass, dispersing the seeds on the wind.

Yellow Mountain Saxifrage

Saxifraga aizoides

SAXIFRAGE FAMILY

This is a sturdy, ground-hugging perennial that forms loose mats or cushions on moist sand, gravel, stream banks and stones in the alpine zone. The upright stems can grow to 10 cm tall, and are crowded with fat, succulent, linear leaves that have an abrupt tip. The leaves are covered in very small, pale hairs. The flowers appear at the tops of the stems, pale yellow and often spotted with orange. The flowers have five petals, which may be ragged at the tips, and there are 10 stamens, with conspicuously large anthers.

Western St. John's Wort

Hypericum scouleri (also *Hypericum formosum*)

ST. JOHN'S WORT FAMILY

This perennial appears in moist places from foothills to the alpine zone and grows to 25 cm tall. Its leaves are opposite, egg-shaped to elliptical, 1–3 cm long, somewhat clasping at the base, and usually have purplish-black dots along the edges. The bright-yellow flowers have five petals and occur in open clusters at the top of the plant. The stamens are numerous, often resembling a starburst.

Lance-Leaved Stonecrop (Spearleaf Stonecrop)

Sedum lanceolatum

STONECROP FAMILY

This fleshy perennial with reddish stems grows up to 15 cm tall on dry, rocky, open slopes and in meadows and rock crevices from low elevations to above timberline. Its numerous, fleshy, alternate leaves are round in cross-section, overlapping and mostly basal. The bright-yellow flowers are star-shaped with sharp-pointed petals, and occur in dense, flat-topped clusters atop short stems.

Round-Leaved Violet (Evergreen Violet)

Viola orbiculata

VIOLET FAMILY

This diminutive flower is an early bloomer, appearing right after the melting snows in moist coniferous forests. Its oval to nearly circular leaves lie flat on the ground and often remain green through the winter. The species name, *orbiculata*, is a reference to the shape of the leaves. The flowers are lemon yellow and have purplish pencilling on the lower three petals. The markings direct insects to the source of the nectar. Candied flowers of this plant are often used for decorating cakes and pastries.

Yellow Wood Violet

Viola glabella

VIOLET FAMILY

This beautiful yellow violet occurs in moist woods, often in extensive patches. There are smooth, serrate, heart-shaped leaves on the upper part of the plant stem. The flowers have very short spurs, and the interior of the side petals often exhibits a white beard. The flower is also commonly referred to as Smooth Violet and Stream Violet.

GLOSSARY

achene: A dry, single-seeded fruit that does not split open at maturity.

alternate: A reference to the arrangement of leaves on a stem where the leaves appear singly and staggered on opposite sides of the stem.

annual: A plant that completes its life cycle, from seed germination to production of new seed, within one year and then dies.

anther: The portion of the stamen (the male portion of a flower) that produces pollen.

axil: The upper angle formed where a leaf, branch or other organ is attached to a plant stem.

basal: A reference to leaves that occur at the bottom of the plant, usually near or on the ground.

berry: A fleshy, many-seeded fruit.

biennial: A plant that completes its life cycle in two years, normally producing leaves in the first year and flowers in the second, before dying.

blade: The body of a leaf, excluding the stalk.

bract: A reduced or otherwise modified leaf that is usually found near the flower of a plant but is not part of the flower. **See also florescence; inflorescence**.

bulb: An underground plant part derived from a short, often rounded shoot that is covered with scales or leaves.

calyx: The outer set of flower parts, usually composed of sepals.

capsule: A dry fruit with more than one compartment that splits open to release seeds.

clasping: In reference to a leaf that surrounds or partially wraps around a stem or branch.

composite inflorescence: A flower-like **inflorescence** of the Composite Family, made up of **ray flowers** and/or **disc flowers**. Where both ray and disc flowers exist, the ray flowers surround the disc flowers.

compound leaf: A leaf that is divided into two or many leaflets, each of which may look like a complete leaf but lacks buds. Compound leaves may have a variety of arrangements.

connate: In reference to leaves where two leaves are fused at their bases to form a shallow cup, often seen in the Honeysuckle Family.

corm: An enlarged base or stem resembling a bulb.

corolla: The collective term for the petals of the flower that are found inside the sepals.

cultivar: A cultivated variety of a wild plant.

cyme: A broad, flat-topped flower arrangement in which the inner, central flowers bloom first.

decumbent: In reference to a plant reclining, or lying on the ground with tip ascending.

disc flower: Any of the small tubular florets found in the central, clustered portion of the flower head of members of the Composite Family; also referred to as "disc florets."

dioecious: Having unisex flowers, where male and female flowers appear on separate plants. **See also monoecious**.

drupe: A fleshy or juicy fruit that covers a single, stony seed inside, e.g., a cherry or a peach.

drupelet: Any one part of an aggregate fruit (like a raspberry or blackberry), where each such part is a fleshy fruit that covers a single, stony seed inside.

elliptical: Ellipse-shaped, widest in the middle. **See also oval**.

elongate: Having a slender form, long in relation to width.

entire: In reference to a leaf edge that is smooth, without teeth or notches.

filament: The part of the stamen that supports the anther. Also can refer to any threadlike structure.

florescence: Generally the flowering part of a plant; the arrangement of the flowers on the stem; also referred to as **inflorescence**. **But see bract**.

floret: One of the small tubular flowers in the central, clustered portion of the flower head of members of the Composite Family; also known as **disc flower**.

follicle: A dry fruit composed of a single compartment that splits open along one side at maturity to release seeds.

fruit: The ripe ovary with the enclosed seeds, and any other structures that enclose it.

glabrous: In reference to a leaf surface, smooth, neither waxy or sticky.

gland: A small organ that secretes a sticky or oily substance and is attached to some part of the plant.

glaucous: Having a fine, waxy, often white coating that may be rubbed off; often characteristic of leaves, fruits and stems.

hood: in reference to flower structure, a curving or folded petal-like structure interior to the petals and exterior to the stamens in certain flowers.

host: In reference to a parasitic or semi-parasitic plant, the plant from which the parasite obtains its nourishment.

inflorescence: Generally the flowering part of a plant; the arrangement of the flowers on the stem; also referred to as **florescence**. **But see bract**.

keel: The two fused petals in flowers that are members of the Pea Family.

lance-shaped: In reference to leaf shape, much longer than wide, widest below the middle and tapering to the tip, like the blade of a lance.

leaflet: A distinct, leaflike segment of a compound leaf.

linear: Like a line; long, narrow and parallel-sided.

lobe: A reference to the arrangement of leaves, a segment of a divided plant part, typically rounded.

margin: The edge of a leaf or petal.

mat: A densely interwoven or tangled, low, ground-hugging growth.

midrib: The main rib of a leaf.

mid-vein: The middle vein of a leaf.

monoecious: A plant having unisex flowers, with separate male and female flowers on the same plant. **See also dioecious**.

nectary: A plant structure that produces and secretes nectar.

node: A joint on a stem or root.

noxious weed: A plant, usually imported, that out-competes and drives out native plants.

oblong: Somewhat rectangular, with rounded ends.

obovate: Shaped like a teardrop.

opposite: A reference to the arrangement of leaves on a stem where the leaves appear paired on opposite sides of the stem, directly across from each other.

oval: Broadly elliptical.

ovary: The portion of the flower where the seeds develop. It is usually a swollen area below the style and stigma.

ovate: Egg-shaped.

palmate: A reference to the arrangement of leaves on a stem where the leaves spread like the fingers on a hand, diverging from a central or common point.

panicle: A branched inflorescence that blooms from the bottom up.

pencilled: Marked with coloured lines, like the petals on Violets.

perennial: A plant that does not produce seeds or flowers until its second year of life, then lives for three or more years, usually flowering each year before dying.

petal: A component of the inner floral portion of a flower, often the most brightly coloured and visible part of the flower.

petiole: The stem of a leaf.

pinnate: A reference to the arrangement of leaves on a stem where the leaves appear in two rows on opposite sides of a central stem, similar to the construction of a feather.

pistil: The female member of a flower that produces seed, consisting of the ovary, the style and the stigma. A flower may have one to several separate pistils.

pistillate: A flower with female reproductive parts but no male reproductive parts.

pollen: The tiny, often powdery male reproductive microspores formed in the stamens and necessary for sexual reproduction in flowering plants.

pome: A fruit with a core, e.g., an apple or pear.

prickle: A small, sharp, spiny outgrowth from the outer surface.

raceme: A flower arrangement that has an elongated flower cluster with the flowers attached to short stalks of relatively equal length that are attached to the main central stalk.

ray flower: One of the outer, strap-shaped petals seen in members of the Composite Family. Ray flowers may surround disc flowers or may comprise the whole of the flower head; also referred to as **ray florets**.

reflexed: Bent backwards, often in reference to petals, bracts or stalks.

rhizome: An underground stem that produces roots and shoots at the nodes.

rosette: A dense cluster of basal leaves from a common underground part, often in a flattened, circular arrangement.

runner: A long, trailing or creeping stem.

saprophyte: An organism that obtains its nutrients from dead organic matter.

scape: A flowering stem, usually leafless, rising from the crown, roots or corm of a plant. Scapes can have a single or many flowers.

sepal: A leaf-like appendage that surrounds the petals of a flower. Collectively the sepals make up the calyx.

serrate: Possessing sharp, forward-pointing teeth.

sessile: Of a plant structure attached directly by its base without a stalk; opposite of "stalked."

shrub: A multi-stemmed woody plant.

simple leaf: A leaf that has a single leaf-like blade, which may be lobed or divided.

spadix: A floral spike with a fleshy or succulent axis usually enclosed in a **spathe**.

spathe: A sheathing **bract** or pair of bracts partly enclosing an **inflorescence** and especially a **spadix** on the same axis.

spike: An elongated, unbranched cluster of stalkless or nearly stalkless flowers.

spine: A thin, stiff, sharp-pointed projection.

spur: A hollow, tubular projection arising from the base of a petal or sepal, often producing nectar.

stalk: The stem supporting the leaf, flower or flower cluster.

stamen: The male member of the flower, which produces pollen; the structure typically consists of an anther and a filament.

staminate: A flower with male reproductive parts but no female reproductive parts

staminode: A sterile stamen.

standard: The uppermost petal of a typical flower in the Pea Family.

stigma: The portion of the pistil receptive to pollination; usually at the top of the style and often sticky or fuzzy.

stolon: A creeping above-ground stem capable of sending up a new plant.

style: A slender stalk connecting the stigma to the ovary in the female organ of a flower.

taproot: A stout main root that extends downward.

tendril: A slender, coiled or twisted filament with which climbing plants attach to their supports.

tepals: Petals and sepals that cannot be distinguished, one from the other.

terminal: At the top of, such as of a stem or other appendage.

terminal flower head: A flower that appears at the top of a stem, as opposed to originating from a leaf axil.

ternate: Arranged in threes, often in reference to leaf structures.

toothed: Bearing teeth or sharply angled projections along the edge.

trailing: Lying flat on the ground but not rooting.

tuber: A thick, creeping underground stem.

tubular: Hollow or cylindrical, usually in reference to a fused corolla.

umbel: A flower arrangement where the flower stalks have a common point of attachment to the stem, like the spokes of an umbrella.

unisexual: Some flowers are unisexual, having either male parts or female parts but not both. Some plants are unisexual, having either male flowers or female flowers but not both.

urn-shaped: Hollow and cylindrical or globular, contracted at the mouth; like an urn.

vacuole: A membrane-bound compartment in a plant that is typically filled with liquid and may perform various functions in the plant.

vein: A small tube that carries water, nutrients and minerals, usually referring to leaves.

viscid: Sticky, thick and gluey.

whorl: Three or more parts attached at the same point along a stem or axis, often surrounding the stem; forming a ring radiating out from a common point.

wings: Side petals that flank the keel in typical flowers of the Pea Family.

INDEX

ABOUT THE AUTHOR

Neil Jennings is an ardent hiker, photographer and outdoorsman who loves "getting down in the dirt" pursuing his keen interest in wildflowers. For 22 years he co-owned a fly-fishing retail store in Calgary, and he has fly-fished extensively, in both fresh and saltwater, for decades. His angling pursuits usually lead him to wildflower investigations in a variety of locations. He taught fly-fishing-related courses in Calgary for over 20 years, and his photographs and writings on that subject have appeared in a number of outdoor magazines. Neil has previously written several volumes published by Rocky Mountain Books, dealing with wildflowers in western Canada, fly-fishing, and hiking venues in southern Alberta. He lives in Calgary, Alberta, with Linda, his wife of over 40 years. They spend a lot of time outdoors together chasing fish, flowers and, as often as possible, grandchildren.